12 RULES OF C

You don't need to be an a

You could be a designer, a
or a teacher.

Everyone is creative. It's a spark that lights us all up.

You don't have to be able to paint or draw. You can begin right now, with what you have in your hands, developing your ideas one by one, as they emerge.

The important thing is to start.

I believe that creativity is a process. Its purpose is to develop self-awareness in you. This is the gold, the true magic of creative life – the power of personal transformation.

Try it and see.

Remember – if you play as a child, the generosity of the child will come out to meet you. As adults we often lose this essential sense of play. It becomes redundant, rusty.

My book attempts to put it back.

12 RULES OF CREATIVITY

MICHAEL ATAVAR

Kiosk Publishing

info@12-rules-of-creativity.com
www.12-rules-of-creativity.com

First published in 2011 by Kiosk Publishing
Second edition 2012

ISBN 978-0-9531073-2-2
A catalogue record for this book is available from the British Library.

Designed by Rose-Innes Associates
Typeset in Trade Gothic

Progredi perservate

Everyone is creative.

CONTENTS

INTRODUCTION

We all face creative blocks.

Many times in my career I've become stuck, not knowing which way to turn. So, confronted by these perennial difficulties, I began to devise different methods for shifting the familiar log-jam and finding a way out.

Some of the techniques are presented in this book.

There's no shame in these creative blocks; we all face them.

From beginner to famous artist, everyone will encounter periods of stuckness in their life. Sometimes it's a brief entanglement, at other times it can be long-term.

The twelve rules in this book will help you navigate these stages of impasse.

The principles I describe here are not intransigent systems, a series of hard and fast rules; rather they are guides, leading you into areas of practice that you hadn't previously considered before – with the purpose of changing your attitude or finding a new perspective.

My advice is always to start, go ahead, do it.

Only by continuing to work with the problem can you address the issue and move through the block to the next level.

Thereby dealing with the challenge in a sympathetic and subtle manner.

At all times trust your intuitive response.

Use the twelve rules presented here as a way of supporting your instinctive sense of your own direction and purpose.

Make a choice, turn the page and begin.

1

OPEN YOUR EYES

- Describe what's
in front of you.
- Record the detail
of everything that
you see.
- Present an original
interpretation of
reality, directed
by your eyes.

OPEN YOUR EYES

Open your eyes. What can you see?

Carry a notepad and pen with you at all times and use it to write about what's around you – words, illustrations, sentences.

Because they come from you, these observations will necessarily be individual, unique.

Every pair of eyes is tuned to an original way of seeing. Each pair of ears hears different things.

The things that you might write in your notepad are –

- The colour of cars.
- Descriptions of faces on the train.
- Snatches of conversation.
- Sunlight.
- Abandoned furniture.
- LED displays.
- The beeps of mobile phones.
- Sunsets.

Don't let some elevated idea of what creativity might be dissuade you from recording what you see every day.

Allow yourself to develop a practice of just looking.

Allow yourself
to develop a
practice of
just looking.

NO LIGHTNING FLASH

The accepted idea of creativity is that ideas come, in a flash, from nowhere – out of the sky like a blast of lightning. The eureka moment.

We think that only geniuses can have good, exciting ideas. I believe that there is no genius. There is no lightning flash.

Instead, creativity is the constellation of many forces – preparation, attention to detail, persistence and self-awareness.

If you tune into these qualities, you will have more ideas, better ideas and perhaps, after many years, you can also have genius ideas.

I have a more prosaic image. The picture I have in my head is of the portable radio.

Using this small, sympathetic device we can tune into the phenomena of the world, turning the dial through the spectrum, in order to find inspiration.

Tune in to allow the free-flowing nature of ideas to develop.

Your creative life is not far off, distant. It's not taking place in Tel Aviv, LA or Berlin.

It's where you are.

It's about –

- You.
- The page.
- What you see.
- What you hear.
- The activity of pen or brush.
- The day.
- The everyday.

It can be activated by the simplest things – repetition, waiting, accumulation, watching.

Often we feel that creative life is beyond us, out there, way off, in a world that we don't yet inhabit. A place reserved for artists, writers, philosophers, designers.

This is not true.

Start saying, 'I'm here. I'm ready to be a creative person.'

Many times, just acknowledging this can be the first step in building a new creative life. Speak it out loud. See what happens when you hear the words coming out of your own mouth.

If you encourage self-reflection in yourself, an open dialogue with the world around you, creativity will find you and support you on your ongoing journey.

Don't delay, start today.

There is no genius. There is no lightning flash.

MARKS

But how do you begin?

The Exercise

Take your pencil and make some marks on the page.

Don't think about what you are doing. Simply move the implement across the paper in a way that feels natural, unaided. After several attempts, go back and see what you have made.

Are there any motifs?

I'm always interested in the doodles that people create – the random scribbles on the page. They are useful clues to the emotional tenor of their personality. Like a Rorschach inkblot test, the doodle can be an instant way of understanding something important about them.

Go ahead – draw some more.

As a creative person, it's always important to begin here with these primitive marks.

Remember, a pencil is a magic wand that you can use to make things appear.

When I went to see an exhibition of Braun products designed by Dieter Rams, what caught my eye were not the artefacts on display, TVs, coffee machines and hi-fi speakers, but a single drawing on the wall.

Here was a homage to the line, as individual as any original voice.

It reminded me that even in the age of the computer, there's still something special about the fluidity of the line on the page. This is an action that the mouse can rarely replicate.

The drawing gave me a direct through-line to the artist's personality, plus a vision back to the start of all mark making, deep in the primitive cave.

Top Tip

Instead of mapping out the whole strategy of a work in advance, do the opposite. Focus on a daily schedule, zooming in on the smallest detail.

Don't aim for perfection; instead allow errors and inconsistencies to develop. Over time, these insignificant parts will actually become the piece.

It's not the value of these individual items that count, rather the application that comes from daily practice and long-term focus.

Take a photograph or make a drawing every 24 hours.

Working this way, as if on automatic pilot, seeing and recording, listening and tuning in, is a good way of developing your creative potential.

A pencil is a magic wand that you can use to make things appear.

TODAY MY EYES SEE

Although it appears chaotic and without boundaries, creativity actually responds to structures, detail and rigour.

Without these factors creative life can't adequately flourish.

Some structures that you could use are –

- Write every day.
- Work without stopping for an hour.
- Record everything that you observe.

Keep a weekly visual log and at the end of a month look back on what you have collected. There's likely to be a surprising amount of connections between the material that you accumulate.

Put all the images out on the floor and see what's there.

- Is there a colour?
- Is there a title?
- Is there a sensation?
- Is there a name?

Create a narrative that might connect all these sections together.

However, you must persist. A month is the minimum amount of time needed for this process. Collect material every day in order to experience a real shift.

The Exercise

Try using the phrase 'Today my eyes see' as a stimulus to creativity, literally describing what's out there in front of you.

When I attempt the exercise I come up with, 'Today my eyes see – white cup, yellow RSVP postcard, grey cloud, pyramid.'

(It can be as abstract as you like.)

Top Tip
The everyday is intrinsically interesting.

Collect daily observations in your notepad.

Use them to generate new material, alerting you to vortices in your creativity, places that you hadn't seen before.

Creativity really responds to structures, detail and rigour.

2

PREPARE THE SPACE

- Adapt the space that you have.
- Make the basic content of your life a source of invention.
- Don’t look outside for inspiration, rather find everything inside you.

PREPARE THE SPACE

I once had a powerful dream in which I was moving TVs and video recorders out of a room. When they were gone, I could clearly see the sparkling floor that had previously been there, hidden under all the mess.

After this dream I began to see preparation as an integral part of creativity. Not just getting ready for something to happen, but the work itself.

Preparation = practice.

We have this idea that creativity must be a product – a book, a performance, an event. I believe that creativity is a process. It might result in some of these external things, but its main purpose is to develop an attitude within ourselves.

Self-reflection is the goal of the creative process.

We are the output.

So –

- Bringing people together can be the work.
- Travelling to a place can be the work.
- Buying a series of materials can be the work.
- Choosing colours can be the work.

12 RULES OF CREATIVITY

You don't need to be an artist to read this book.

You could be a designer, a student, a businessman or a teacher.

If these catapult you into a creative process then that's OK.

Be playful, move objects around, create space, enjoy form.

When I first went to the Zen temple, I was given the task of cleaning the communal toilets and polishing the glass panelled doors. I later discovered that this is standard practice for novices.

At first I was horrified by the idea of cleaning up after other people. However, after a while I came to like this task. I began to enjoy it. I wanted to make my glass door shine like a mirror.

I realised that I could begin a project by meticulously organising the space and making it ready.

Preparing is enough. In fact, this is the work.

Twenty Ways Of Preparing The Space

- Clean the space.
- Use a brush to sweep away what's been there before.
- Open the windows.
- Make a series of loud sounds.
- Or whisper into the corners.
- Remove excess furniture.
- Lift any boxes or bags off the floor.

- Remove old or defunct equipment, long past its sell-by date.
- Remove unnecessary papers.
- Clear what's under the bed.
- Wash the doors, the floors, the walls, the windows.
- Wash yourself.
- Wash your ears, your eyelids, your nose, your hands.
- Buy new light bulbs.
- Paint the entrance.
- Add mirrors.
- Whitewash the walls.
- Strip everything back, ready to begin.
- Light a single candle.
- Watch it burn down to nothing.

I've always been inspired by the example of artist Carl Andre.

He doesn't have a studio or an office. All he uses is a notepad, a telephone and a copy of the Yellow Pages. His process takes place entirely in his head. Once he has conceived of the work, he translates it into material form by ordering cut quantities of slate, wood or concrete from his building suppliers. Then the work is assembled in the gallery.

Andre's 'Equivalent VIII' (better known as 'The Tate Bricks') is a good example of this low-fi, highly imaginative, non-intrusive, modular approach to creativity.

Top Tip
In order to start a new work, clean the space from top to bottom. Use salt water. Get on your hands and knees and scrub the windows and floors.

Remember, any place can be made to be creative – a train carriage, your kitchen table, a seat in the doctor's surgery.

If you are connected with your creativity, this can be the only space you need to flourish.

Self-reflection
is the goal of
the creative
process.

THE AUTOMATIC

Perhaps you are already feeling that creativity is something special, something that you have no access to?

If so, I encourage you to continue.

Creativity requires no fancy apparatus. It needs no computer, no office, no assistant. It's merely a series of processes that we can all use, in order to grow our creative potential.

A pencil and a piece of paper are all you need.

Try the following exercise.

The Exercise

Write for one hour without stopping. Make as many mistakes as you like. Allow spelling errors, crossings out and poor handwriting.

Later, assess what you have written.

You can apply this technique to any area of creativity. Painting, drawing, performance – do it for an hour, without thinking what's happening. Just let the form emerge.

If you don't know what to write, record –

- Your name.
- Your age.
- Your first day at school.
- Your city.
- Your ambitions.
- Your view from the window.

If possible, keep writing these over and over again.

Even try dancing for sixty minutes. If you find this arduous at first, move as slowly as possible through a series of minimal moves, just changing your hand positions.

If necessary, allow exhaustion to aid you. Keep working until you are over-tired. Repeat endlessly, on a loop, like an improvisation, until you locate a gem, a small piece of an idea that you want to develop.

When I made my daily writing piece 'beginagain' (2010), I set strict structures around the work. Each day, by midnight, I would write and upload, to a public space, what I had made in the previous 24 hours.

The relentless pace of the piece forced me to make choices that couldn't be subsequently altered.

Instead of inhibiting me, the process actually allowed a large body of work to develop, piece by piece, in front of my eyes

I also believe that if there's no potential for exposure, it's unlikely that something interesting is happening.

Embarrassment is key.

Working automatically allowed this to happen.

If you push yourself beyond what you are used to, beyond the limits of what you know, into the unknowable, ideas will come.

Top Tip
Improvise using yourself as the basic material.

If you push yourself beyond what you are used to, ideas will come.

BASIC MATERIALS

I strongly believe in the unique person and the potential of their outsider status.

The isolated individual has the possibility of channelling their own personality into a special form of creativity. In the outsider's world, years on the margins can be just what's needed to inspire their creative endeavours.

If you haven't had this useful opportunity of being excluded, the archetype of the outsider is a helpful one to consider.

Explore it.

You don't need to completely inhabit this role in order to be creative. Play with it. Step inside, then out.

For the first ten years of my creative life I had little output. However, in retrospect, these sparse years were a vital part of my education. I learned how to make products from the most basic of materials.

This bare bones approach served me well. When I started to make work with computers, I didn't employ complicated software, but instead used the most obvious programming tools, to make simple but sophisticated online products, defining a style that ran in opposition to other things in the marketplace.

This is always a good way of working.

Use any obsession or deviation from the crowd to signal an original way of thinking – a spark or a flaw that can draw an audience's attention. Many times it's their warped quality that really makes someone stand out.

Personally, I like the potential of old technologies, long abandoned by the mainstream.

I'd like to see an artist make a creative piece with fax machines, sending messages out to offices every Friday – in the same way that John Cage used the primitive form of the radio in 'Radio Music' to create a very complex environment.

'Outsider' can therefore also be uncertain, irregular, anomalous, unique.

The Exercise

Remain in any place for a minimum of one hour. Play the role of outsider. Spend no money.

What happens?

Use a spark or a flaw to draw an audience's attention.

3

PLAY

- Play like a child.
- Use this perspective to look at the world from a new angle.
- Build a relationship with your playful side through the use of games and toys.

PLAY

On my desk I have kids' toys from the 70s.

I once had an artist who came to see me, struggling with many choices. Using the toys on my desk, she assembled a plan, using the pieces to add walls and boundaries around her work, barriers that made the task easier.

Each element represented a challenge, a frontier.

In our lives we are encouraged to abandon play, to submit to adult conformity. However, what is art making or creativity itself but the same activities that once occupied us as children?

Develop your ability to play in order to strengthen your creative potential.

The Exercise

Get on the floor and play with toys.

The floor is the best place to shift your perception back to childhood. Stretch out, luxuriating in the extra dimension that the carpeted world gives you, a place in your imagination as wide as a forest, the Steppes, a battlefield, the cosmos.

Build –

- A castle.
- A garden.
- A ship.
- A bird.
- A planet.
- A city.
- A forcefield.
- A river.

Make these items out of cardboard, egg boxes or bottle tops.

When creatively blocked, get into the habit of lying on the floor. Note how your worldview changes. Does it not feel enticing, dangerous, exciting?

Alternatively, if this feels too difficult, simply get out of your chair and lie on the floor. Put your back against the ground and your palms flat on the carpet. Take some moments to breathe deeply.

Don't worry how long you are able to stay there. Simply rest. Feel supported by the ground. Let your mind wander back to your first memories.

Take away the tensions of adulthood. Open yourself up to the child.

I'm often struck by how my own creativity is simply a constellation of things that happen to me within a given time-frame.

For example, when making a new work 'Look At This', I gathered together in a sequence a group of current ideas.

Instead of looking for an over-arching narrative, I slowly assembled the parts, avoiding any sense of order.

I knew that if I continued to play, the bigger theme would naturally emerge within the process, over time.

The content could be the subject of the work.

It didn't need anything else.

Top Tip
Think about making a written agreement with yourself, a simple pact to set aside a minimum of ten minutes each day to play.

(I include a version of this contract on the next page.)

This daily commitment, activated every 24 hours, driven by your will, could really change things.

Anything can be achieved in just these first few minutes.

Contract For Play

I, ______________________ commit to 10/20/30* minutes of play each day for 30/60/90* days.
(* Delete as appropriate.)

Signed: Dated:

When creatively blocked, get into the habit of lying on the floor. Note how your worldview changes.

TUNING IN

Creativity is nothing but tuning in.

Use the image of the dial on a portable radio to pick up the frequencies of good ideas. These ideas are everywhere. In a busy city they fly here and there, bouncing off the walls and pavements.

Gather them as you tune in your radio aerial.

In 1997 I made a project, 'DIY', for TV's Channel 4, a film in which I followed the now extinct path of famous writer Joe Orton.

In order to listen to the past, I used a glass placed against a wall. This mediumistic technique allowed me to explore a range of feelings outside the ones that were normally accessible. Rather than a small slice of the bandwidth, I could tune in to a 360 degree spectrum.

However, most of what I was listening to, I now realise was material coming from inside me.

Our imagination is all.

I believe that if we stay in one place, watching and waiting, inspiration always comes. The temptation is to seek out many sources, to stimulate us, but it's not really necessary.

- A colour
- An enquiry
- An observation
- A tone

is all that's needed.

Try any single idea, well executed, to good effect.

Top Tip

In my cupboard I have a white box filled with the notepads of the last few years. When I think of clearing out these objects, I remember that they represent my ongoing commitment to a practice of looking and can't be easily discarded.

So I continue to hold on to them.

Some of the ideas within these pages will develop over many years before they find their final form.

Think of your notepad as the limit of your creative life. The small changes and ideas that happen there are the focus of creativity.

There is no big idea.

What's seen there is, in fact, the practice.

If we stay in one place, watching and waiting, inspiration always comes.

TENT

Creativity is a method for investigating the self.

- It's where you are.
- It's what you look at.
- It's who you are.

What do you have control of apart from yourself?

For example, with this book, if you are struggling with the text, simply give up.

Work only with the tension inside you, always coming back to your immediate resources. If that doesn't happen, abandon any plans for making creative work until you've finished reading the last page of this volume.

Sometimes it's necessary just to stop.

If you look at creativity as if it were a temporary structure, fixed to very limited outputs on a day-to-day basis, it's a good way of avoiding the paranoia generated by over-ambitious creative goals.

Instead, dig deep. Excavate where you are.

Like an archaeological site, build a tent over the ground in order to examine what you find.

When it's done, when your process is complete, pack up the tent and move on.

The artistic landscape is always dotted with these research tents. Sometimes you can join them up, congregate with others, in order to cross-pollinate or find common goals.

I like the image of the temporary tents – it feels light, easy, portable.

Creativity can flourish in this atmosphere of adaptability and change. If it doesn't work here, today, simply pick up sticks and move on.

What To Pack In Your Creativity Kit

- A pen.
- Some paper to write on.
- Water.
- A calendar, for day-to-day goals
- A microphone, to amplify.
- A length of tape.
- A penknife to cut through.
- Batteries.
- Felt-tips.
- Sandwiches for a longer stay.
- A cheap camera.

If none of these help, try my recipe to sustain you for longer, artistic-led nights at home.

Fish Finger Sandwich

Take two small slices of white crusty bread and spread both pieces thickly with cream cheese. Layer one side with an over-sized piece of Romaine lettuce or a scoop of watercress. On top, place three well-grilled fish fingers and sandwich together. Add a twist of ground black pepper or a squeeze of lemon.

Cut in half.

Don't worry if this sandwich falls apart. It's meant to – bits of broken fish and breadcrumbs gathered up in your fingers from the plate.

The joy of a fish finger sandwich is that it takes you beyond the boundaries of good taste into a childhood space where everything is incoherent but essentially alright.

Creativity takes root in messy procedures.

Creativity takes root in messy procedures.

INTERVIEW YOURSELF

If in doubt, interview yourself.

What you are doing, through this exercise, is taking the temperature. Essentially, you hope to find out about your current interests and so work more intensively on these areas of your creative practice.

The Exercise

Use the following questions.

When you take this test, write out your answers by hand in your notepad. Give your replies honestly, without the slightest suggestion of irony.

It's a real interview.

- What's your name?
- Where is your home?
- Where do you belong?
- What motivates you?
- What currently are your themes/obsessions?
- What's your relationship to the crowd?
- Name three colours that you like.
- Name three animals that you like.
- Name three numbers that you like.
- Describe your perfect day.
- Describe your preferred journey.
- Day time or night time?

- Roads or air?
- Mountains or sea?
- Who is your favourite artist?
- Who is your favourite writer?
- Who is your favourite musician?
- What's your favourite beginning?
- What's your favourite ending?
- Name your preferred café.
- Name your preferred designer.
- Name your preferred disco.
- What's your motto?
- What's your philosophy?
- Who are your friends?
- Tell me one thing about yourself that no one knows.

When you have finished, read through your answers and see if anything leaps out at you.

- Are you buoyant/melancholy?
- Are you strident/reclusive?
- Are you negative/optimistic?

What's the tone, the temperature of your answers?

Writing these responses won't solve your problems, but it might encourage a quality of self-reflection in you that's hopeful and optimistic.

Use this exercise to explore ways of talking about your work. Learn to dramatise your own process.

Top Tip

Call yourself 'Director', 'Film Maker' or 'Writer'.

If you talk about your work, using the language of successful creatives, some magic happens and your audience will begin to take you seriously and accept your narrative at face value.

Ideas form through action. If you don't harness them, they will evaporate, disappear.

Use the name you call yourself as the place that you are moving to.

'Creative' is the land that you intend to inhabit.

Ideas form
through action.
If you don't
harness them,
they will
evaporate,
disappear.

4

USE IMAGES

- Use images as a creative shorthand.
- Don't be concerned if you can't draw.
- Engage with the paper in a limitless way, organising form and colour, tone and line.

USE IMAGES

We have all got caught up in the idea that words are the only way of articulating ideas. This is not true. These tools are useful in exploring certain concepts but there are many other ways of describing things –

- Maps.
- Diagrams.
- 3-D drawings.
- Charts.

Keep a notepad with you for such explorations. Don't think that a pen and paper are only effective for writing sentences. The felt-tip is a fluid tool, allowing your eye to connect with the page in very dynamic ways. If your creativity gets stuck, draw the problem – feelings, conflicts, sensations.

Try it.

Drawing is a highly effective technique for unlocking creative blocks.

So –

- Press hard for anger.
- Fill up the whole page with one word to show its dominance.
- Make slight, expressive marks to suggest lightness.
- Or use the page folded like a piece of origami.

Remember, you can actively participate in your own solution through the use of images. They are highly effective, practical and cheap to output.

They cost you nothing.

In times of creative frustration, always have a pen and notepad on your desk. Don't think about it, just draw. Later, dissect what you have made.

For example, if I get stuck, I rapidly execute a series of squiggles in order to download to the page all the material that's filling up my head, thereby letting it go.

Similarly, you can achieve the same effect now by standing up suddenly and moving around the room in an unexpected way.

What do you notice?

Remember – sometimes these observations ARE the piece.

Also, you don't need to be able to draw to work with images. Just imagine it in your head. Picture it inside you, in as much detail as you need to make it real.

After all, a written 'to do' list is always uninspiring. Who wants to attempt to work through a long, exhaustive, boring series of chores?

Instead draw –

- Crates.
- Boulders.
- Diggers.
- Beaches.
- Chocolate boxes.
- Gold dust.
- Sticks.
- Streets.
- Catapults.
- Cherry stones.
- Glitter.
- Frescos.
- Cranes.
- Flamboyant flowers.
- Robbers.
- Dirt.
- Mirrors.
- Waves.

Make lines across the page.

Follow one of these as long as it will go.

If your creativity gets stuck, draw the problem – feelings, conflicts, sensations.

IS THAT ME?

I remember using this exercise in a workshop that I ran for artists, within the unlikely setting of a council high-rise block.

However, the following Gestalt technique is highly effective for testing out the limits of personality.

I've used it all the way through my career.

The Exercise

Choose some images that you feel drawn to.

Don't think about this too much – simply pick them up wherever they appear – in glossy magazines, free postcards, ads in newspapers, flyers.

It could be a photograph, a drawing or a painting.

At the end of the week, lay the pictures out in front of you on the floor and select one that attracts your attention.

Remove it from the group.

Describe the detail of this image as if it was you. Use the 'I' word. For example, if it's an image of a rock, you could say, 'I'm cold', 'I have been created over many years' or 'I can be thrown at a glass house'.

Find as many possibilities as you can.

It's remarkable how this simple exercise can help locate lost parts of your personality or future potential locked inside the unconscious.

In my workshop, I recall that one participant chose an image of a rose.

He carefully explored the different parts of this picture – its delicacy and thorniness – providing reflective insights into his current state.

Flower, petal, stem.

Use images to add wildness and unpredictability to your creativity, encouraging new pathways of the personality, places that you couldn't see before.

They are every place that you look.

Use images to add wildness and unpredictability to your creativity, encouraging new pathways of the personality.

LASSO

My own visual art practice came out of a simple desire to provide images to promote individual pieces of work – on postcards and posters.

Gradually these functional, background items took centre stage and became the work.

Even now, a photograph will often provide the spark for a project.

(I've worked with salt, clouds, knives and blue skies; boulders, stars, tight-ropes and super powers.)

Visual clues like these offer me instant entry points into the project, giving an overall and immediate sense of the completed work.

From the picture I can progress backwards into the thing.

Likewise, I believe that there is no creative problem that can't be solved by the use of images and the pointed delivery of your imagination.

If you get stuck in a hole, use the following visual technique to pull you out.

The Exercise

In your mind's eye, cradle a rope lasso in your hands and then cast it outwards towards the object of your desire – a person, a job, a house. Draw it towards you, firmly reeling in the item.

In your imagination, keep eye contact with the object. Pull it vigorously, as a cowboy might capture a steer. The future is out there, waiting for you.

This 'lasso' technique is a good way of focusing on what you want and taking a determined path towards your goal.

But here are some more...

Twenty Other Visualisations For Unsticking Yourself

These simple exercises can be practised at any time – on a train, in a launderette or on a packed bus.

Simply create the image in your head –

- Build a doorway.
- Imagine a garden.
- Cut yourself out using imaginary scissors.
- Become invisible.
- Swim to an island where things are possible.
- Make something magically better.
- Stand under a waterfall to cleanse yourself.

- Plant your feet on the ground.
- Cross a bridge.
- Meet your foe face to face.
- Build a wall.
- Lock a door to the past.
- Create a protective forcefield.
- Climb a mountain to get an overview.
- Shrink someone.
- Create an enveloping, safe light.
- Try flying above the ground.
- Travel back in time.
- Unlock a barely used room.
- Lower the curtain on an event.

(Or develop your own images.)

Top Tip

Many times, even if your idiom is language, it's useful to work with non-writing-based systems.

The picture will take you directly into the feeling, in a way that pages of text cannot achieve.

For example, if you are writing a novel, have an image above your desk – a photograph that encapsulates all the ideas that you are trying to articulate.

Have an image above your desk – a photograph that encapsulates all the ideas that you are trying to articulate.

5

DO THE OPPOSITE

- Use your outsider status as a tool.
- Don’t be intimidated by the mainstream.
- Original ideas come from the overturning of conventional values and opinions.

DO THE OPPOSITE

Once an artist came to see me.

Many of the statements that he made, I thought that the opposite might be true. 'I love my work', 'I'm interested in the future' etc. My instinct was that he was not revealing what he really thought.

This gave me the idea that it's useful to work with the contrary of what we believe in, to see where it might take us.

No creative solution makes sense.

All solutions are chaotic, off-centre and dangerous – until they become part of the mainstream. Then they become normalised through familiarity and use.

But until that time, you are working with the opposite in order to encourage surprise in your work.

The life of the artist is about using the reverse of what's normally present, making something no one else can see. If everyone is looking one way, at one particular thing, one problem, you need to look in the opposite direction, at contrary things.

Encourage your ability to find value in what others discard –

- Litter.
- Free gifts.
- Packaging.
- £1 items.
- Dust.
- Plastic toys.

Develop a mindset that doesn't seek out expensive solutions to difficult problems. Use the opposite to resensitise you to a world that you have forgotten.

For example, if you go to work every day, fighting with commuters for any extra space, try the following exercise.

The Backwards Day Technique

For one day, instead of doing things forwards, try everything backwards.

So –

8am	Go to bed for an hour.
9am	Don't wash.
10am	Prepare dinner.
11am	Eat dinner.
12pm	Watch TV for an hour.
1pm	Watch TV for another hour.
2pm	Go swimming or attend the gym.
3pm	Go to work.
4pm	Write some texts.

5pm	Have lunch.
6pm	Drink coffee.
7pm	Make phone calls to your boss.
8pm	Check your calendar.
9pm	Travel somewhere.
10pm	Have a shower.
11pm	Eat breakfast.
12am	Wake up.

In this exercise, what you are attempting to do is disrupt yourself, put your identity into a zone where creativity comes more naturally to you.

Creative thinking is available on any street, in all cities – even in packed commuter carriages at rush hour, on the way to work. However, you can't normally see it because you are following the crowd, all moving in the same direction.

The 'backwards day' technique offers a different perspective.

Top Tip

Giving an idea a title can be a unique form of creativity.

The concept already exists, or is there in the zeitgeist, but no one has identified it before. Your job is merely to name it.

Here are some suggestions –

- The Horizontal.
- Oblique Purpose.
- The Cuts.
- Your Imagination.
- Process A.

Etc.

(All my own fantasy art movements.)

Similarly, perhaps, even though you don't realise it, your project is already finished. You've done all the work. Your job is merely to recognise that fact and to give the completed item a name.

Good luck.

Encourage your ability to find value in what others discard.

SWITCH PLACES

If I get stuck, I often try to experience other registers, different modalities.

The idea that we are all simply working in one methodology is not a useful one for developing creativity. Try something that you have no knowledge of, to offer a new perspective on what you can do.

For example, if you are the singer in a band, try the drums. If you are a bass player, temporarily take up the violin. If you are a keyboard player, use the bongos.

Often our lack of skill gives us insight into a process that a more adept user might not see. A novice might try something a more skilled practitioner would never attempt, like splashing the canvas with paint or playing an incomplete series of chords.

These, in fact, might be good things to try...

Cultivate your ability to switch places frequently –

- If it doesn't work in words, draw it.
- If it's not successful as music, try and model it in 3-D.
- If it doesn't work as dance, paint it.

This principle has been well described in Edward de Bono's 'Six Thinking Hats', a sophisticated variation on the idea of changing forms or switching places.

Top Tip

Be open about the fact that you can see an obstacle exists. Be smart. If in doubt, name any problem. Make it available for discussion. The insightful person uses the difficulty itself to explore the limits of any problem, thereby detonating the issue.

Don't deny feedback from any source. You might get useful suggestions or, better still, a good idea for free.

Twenty Ways To Shift Forms

- Swap places with your boss.
- Let everyone around the table have an equal say.
- Swap positions in meetings to encourage another view.
- Circulate the chair at events.
- Have a permanent suggestion box.
- Accept others' ideas on a regular basis. Have one think tank session per month.
- Allow interruptions.
- Have a creative object, an item of clothing that you wear when you need to discover a new idea.
- Make it a pair of shoes, a tie or a brooch. Invest this item with some magic.
- Use the clothing if you get stuck.
- Swap places, swap desks, swap hours.

- Redecorate the office or the workroom.
- Buy a quality water cooler or coffee machine to encourage casual groupings and ideas' exchange.
- Challenge received opinions and basic hierarchies.
- Have meetings where you look exclusively at visual materials.
- Put up pictures in the staff room. Rotate the visual landscape.
- Make a check-in a prerequisite for any meeting.
- Make a check-out a prerequisite for any meeting.
- Use colour to encourage mood.
- Place toys on your desk.

Novelty is a useful choice for stimulating a creative life.

Develop your creativity by becoming a friend of the gimmicky – novelty is often the frontier in culture for new technological ideas, a place where innovation happens.

Integrate the odd, the misplaced, the incomplete, the abandoned.

Use tongue in cheek magic.

Shift often to experience other registers, different modalities.

LISTENING SPACE

There's little that you can do to force creative ideas.

Instead, create a space where your whole activity is directed towards watching and waiting. If nothing arrives, keep repeating this activity, if necessary alone, until something shifts.

This might not be dramatic. It could be just that your perception alters slightly. You might notice something different on the street – that's enough.

For example, if what you observe are scraps of paper, then collect them. If it's dust, assemble that. Place the pieces in your dust museum. Remember, nothing is too minor a subject for creativity.

Recently, I met an artist who was interested in the idea of working with presence. As an exercise, I asked her to bring her sense of being here into all her interactions – including the one that she was having with me, right at that moment, and to record those meetings in a daily log.

After all, what else could she do but integrate her difficulty, her fight to be present, into the work?

I believe that the mystic Gurdjieff was right when he stated that there's only a limited amount of understanding or creative thinking in the world.

What there is available to us can be accessed here, today.

Any book that says the creative artist can be expanded is largely a fraud. Creativity doesn't come from expansion but from the individual boundaries that spur us to work within our own limits.

There is no magic formula that will make you more creative. In fact, we each have a limited amount of knowledge, inspiration, acuity and perseverance. Nothing that you can do will extend that.

Scraps and portions, limits and boundaries – these are the material core of creativity.

It's also useful to remember André Breton's adage that everything can be found on the street.

If I were making a piece of work, I might look here, on the pavement, where energy constellates, keeping my eyes and ears alert to the minor key changes of the city. The street is where you are less protected, and so open to phenomena when they strike.

Most of the things I include in my daily writing exercises are microscopic descriptions of urban life, as they are received by my own senses: transport details, weather, light qualities, food prices.

The Exercise

Detune your eyes slightly, allowing you to focus less on what's directly in front of you and more on the general feeling around you.

Make your eyesight a blur.

With less visual stimulus to distract you, concentrate instead on your other senses. Pay particular attention to hearing and aural stimulus.

What can you see now?

Limits and boundaries – these are the material core of creativity.

WORKING WITH SHADOWS

I've seen enough of creativity to realise that working with the imagination is often dangerous material.

At all times in the creative process, great care must be taken to protect your soft and vulnerable qualities.

Often these feelings can be abused by people who don't care for experimentation or curiosity.

In the modern world, risk and play are commodities in short supply. Always support and encourage yourself – as a first line of defence.

- Invite limited feedback only.
- Be prepared.
- Gather excellent networks around you.
- Expose only what's necessary.
- Be vigilant.

Remember, with the exposure of art can come shame.

And shame is unpredictable, vituperative.

In this version of art, all creativity is a rehearsal of the abandonment that once filled our early life. We engage in creativity in order to converse with the primitive feelings of rejection that used to occupy a large part of our childhood world.

This wounding keeps happening to us, in adult life, until we learn how to break free.

(Perhaps this is the down side to 'outsider status'.)

If you are making work that is experimental, remember that you will rarely be congratulated for it. Instead, you might find yourself marginalised, available for criticism by the mainstream.

Top Tip
Creativity is always high risk.

Work only with small parts of the personality, ones that you feel happy to show.

In any challenging creative situation, imagine temporary walls around you or an invisible forcefield that can protect you from harsh words.

Creative life is fraught with dangers.

This technique allows the rocks to just bounce off.

At all times in the creative process, great care must be taken to protect your soft and vulnerable qualities.

BEING HERE

Usually we don't know where we are going.

The rules in this book are mechanisms that we can use, as creative people, to fool ourselves into believing that we know what we are doing – and thus continue.

'Daily Writing', 'The Value Of Play, 'The Role Of Drawing', 'Disruptions In Form', 'Working Backwards' – remember what you have learned so far.

Sometimes creativity is nothing other than opening your eyes and recording what you see.

Be authentic – after all, who can argue with that?

Also by stepping into the space and making yourself visible, you naturally help to disperse any feelings that you might have of containment and fear.

It's a form of magic.

Try it.

Focus on being here, addressing what is and acting unafraid.

The shadows don't automatically disappear, but rather, by describing a problem or admitting that one exists, you naturally move ahead.

So with that in mind...

Are you –

- Sad.
- Confident.
- Alive.
- Exhausted.
- Angry.
- Shy.
- Purposeful?

Tell me how you feel.

Sometimes
creativity is
nothing other
than recording
what you see.

WHAT'S AT THE END OF FIVE

Some creative ideas are practical solutions to simple problems, like how to end, how to generate material, how to get started.

If you are stuck, give something a title that describes exactly what it is, like 'What's At The End Of Five', the name of this section.

Don't be afraid of saying the obvious.

Other possibilities are –

- 'One Hundred Interviews.'
- 'An Invitation To Leave Something.'
- '24 Hours Recorded In A Day.'

(By the way these are all titles.)

Get the idea?

Sometimes the old Zen adage really works – first thought, best thought. Why revise anything? Use your instinct to direct you to the most simple and childlike solution available to your complex, exhausting problem.

Inevitably it will be the right answer.

Use your instinct
to direct you to
the most simple
and childlike
solution
available.

6

DEVELOP FAILURE

- Allow yourself to make mistakes.
- Be inspired by risk taking.
- Build a conversation with action that allows you to keep moving, through a series of possible futures.

DEVELOP FAILURE

Boulders crash through your window and land on the page – there they remain, intransigent and immobile.

You feel stuck, not knowing what to do next, which choice to make or how to proceed. These rocks fill up the whole of your imagination, flattening you, making a trap.

It's hard to see these monsters as anything other than bad news.

However, they are not so terrible...

In my creative life, I now see the periods of inactivity, or failure, as necessary for the development of my own internal processes. In fact, these times are rich in sensibility and meaning.

So, don't panic.

The blocks that I describe here will finally disappear.

Wave after wave of creativity comes. You ride it, when the inspiration is there and consolidate when it shrinks back. It's an adventure. Sometimes we have a flood of ideas, at other times there are more meagre pickings.

Learn to value both.

In your mind, try shrinking the boulders. Or, if they are asteroids, attempt to retrace their path to the distant place that they came from. Here, in the terrible void of the imagination, the space that you so fear so much, you might find some clues as to their emergence.

Shadows, projections, mists, phantoms.

The troubling reality, one that's really hard to face, is that these rocks can actually be dismantled chip by chip.

Because they are really YOU.

(Or perceptions from you.)

Use the techniques you will learn in this section of the book to remove these fortress rocks, rolling the boulders out of the way, battling with the unlikely qualities of perception, kindness, psychological nuance and awareness.

If you accept that blocks are an inevitable part of your creative process, they will immediately always disappear.

Battle with
the unlikely
qualities of
perception,
kindness,
psychological
nuance and
awareness.

MAGNIFY THE NEGATIVE

Faced with the multiple choices of the modern world, it's often easier to give up and not pursue any creative path at all.

I find that this is a problem that concerns most people – where to focus their attention in a dwindling landscape.

An artist once came to see me with five projects on the table, each one going back several years.

Where should she begin?

I said that she should magnify the most negative element until it's enlarged, filling the whole space. This giant balloon of confused energy is where new ideas will emerge.

Feel the tension...and stay with it.

However, as clever human beings, we are more likely to surround ourselves with complicated levels of denial in order to stop ourselves from having to begin.

This is where the pain is – in starting. Unfortunately, within creative life, it can't be avoided. We are always beginning, again and again, every day.

Actually, any product that you make is an amplification of you, nothing more and nothing less, just as this book is simply an extension of me, like a prosthetic arm, used to handle nuclear materials.

I hold my book up in workshops and lectures and say unequivocally, 'This is me'.

It's part of my DNA.

The Exercise

So, in effect, what I'm saying is tell me, in detail, about your life. Write down a hundred things that you know about yourself.

Use these minor, revelatory images to start a practice.

Any product
that you make
is simply an
amplification
of you.

REDUCE YOUR OPTIONS

Creativity is thought of as uncontrollable and chaotic – however, on the contrary, I find that it responds well to restrictive structures.

In fact, limits are good for stimulating the creative process. A tight schedule is a useful way of combating inertia.

This book was mostly written on the way to work, where I did my office job, five days a week. Each day I boarded the overground in the suburbs and would write until I reached the terminus in the city centre.

On the train, I would make notes or scribble clues in my notepad. Successive days, jumbled around, facts and figures mixed up, often made sense together on the page – the boundary of the single leaf providing a framework to hold several key concepts inside.

The packed conditions were actually a part of the project.

The endless brick walls of the city always appear to mediate against creativity. However, I'm not so sure. I believe that they are the necessary limits that we need to work within in order to zigzag towards creativity. The twists and turns of creative process emerge in relationship to these dangers.

The resources inside you – self-awareness of your own process – are the best method of magnetising creativity. If this includes periods of difficulty, I don't regard that as problematic. In fact, it's a plus.

Integrate these challenges into your creative life, adding complexity along the way.

Top Tip

Don't aspire to being exclusively a writer or an artist. You will spend too many days looking out of the window. Instead, invest in a variety of experiences, both creative and mundane.

A good mixture of these two approaches is the best method.

I've also often fallen foul of the 'rules' of creativity by making work that is impossible to contain within one single format – writing, performance, books, visual art.

Sometimes the relationship between these diverse and contradictory forms is complicated. But for me that's OK.

However, in 2008 when I was in São Paulo, I noticed that many of the visual artists exhibiting there were also making music in live bands. This struck me as a very non-European way of approaching creativity – populist and refreshing.

But to get back to structures...

The Exercise

Reduce your options by making a list of five limits that might inhibit your practice.

For example –

- Make it in one room.
- Make it within your body.
- Make it without sound.
- Make it no longer than ten minutes.
- Make it without money.

(Create your own five rules.)

Set yourself impossible targets then rigorously apply these strictures to your output and see what happens.

Make a body of work based on these structures.

Recently, when I was with an artist, I created one of these rule lists. As we sat in the meeting room, discussing the material, a child appeared at the door, blowing a pretend trumpet made out of a rolled-up piece of cheap paper.

I realised that 'the child' was pushing into the space, metaphorically and physically, challenging this artist to integrate the chaotic into his practice.

The clever creative takes these phenomenological events, grounded in the real world, and turns them into tools, inviting outside elements into the process.

Surely one of the rules that we created that day should have been 'Include The Child'.

Self-awareness of your own process is the best method for magnetising creativity.

CONFUCIUS SAYS

If you are stuck, one good trick is to inhabit the style or format of another creative.

Whilst copying this other person, it won't be possible to exactly repeat the other's mannerisms so, through your mistakes, you will create another useful approach – your own style.

This person could be a historical figure or someone still alive.

Build your work as if –

- Confucius
- HAL
- Wittgenstein
- A Japanese geisha
- Hulme

were making it.

(These are just some of my suggestions.)

All period material is fuel. Mozart and Courrèges, Kant and computers, cave paintings and Mary Quant. A splintered and stylised hybrid might fire your process or give you permission to continue.

Try mimicking –

- A Vermeer in pencil.
- Biro drawings of various plastic supermarket shopping bags.
- Eighteenth century techniques with modern subject matter.
- Portraits in blood.

Often you can add to this technique by actually using the equipment of another artist.

Borrow their brushes, keyboard, pen or microphone. What difference does it make? Is it possible to channel the feelings of this creative artist through their toolbox?

Use them as a mediumistic transfer, speaking through their voice, in their tone, with their ideas.

What does that allow you to do?

If necessary, hire some equipment, for a week, to get another perspective on a practice that you have become overly familiar with.

For example, if you are a visual artist, rent a paint-spraying machine to cover your canvasses by a different method. Or if you are a musician, hire a set of drums, even if you can't play them.

Top Tip
Choose an unpredictable new collaborator. If possible, work with someone younger than yourself. Allow them free rein to remake a part of your work.

Does this fill you with anxiety?

Dip into fear occasionally in order to encourage a progressive take on your creativity, particularly if you have been making work for some years.

Don't make it easy for yourself.

You will get nowhere.

Don’t make it easy for yourself. You will get nowhere.

A4

Another good rule for reducing your options is to work with the basic elements that you can easily find around you in your home – paper, a radio, some pens, a chair.

The Exercise

For this exercise all you need is a sheaf of A4.

(A pile of paper.)

On your desk, place the pack to your left and put the first piece into your typewriter. Type on it and stack the completed page to your right. Keep going until all the written pages are neatly piled up and the pack of paper is empty.

This is your work.

(Adapt for any recent technology.)

I've always liked the image in the film 'The Shining' of the unfathomable and empty novel that Jack obsessively writes.

It reminds me of the creative process. Sometimes nothing emerges, sometimes everything comes. However, it's necessary to be there, at the right time, at your desk, fingers poised, when inspiration does find you.

By being there you make it arrive.

Top Tip
Another way of achieving the same result is to shrink your work down to its component parts, noting any surprises or deficiencies that you find there.

Try the A4 test.

Reduce any idea to the size of an A4 sheet of paper, whether an image or a piece of text. Strip out any unnecessary padding.

Hold it up in front of others.

Does your idea still work in this limited form?

By being there
you make
inspiration
arrive.

7

CHECK-IN

- Create a listening space inside you.
- Find time for this inner resource every day.
- Use it to access a daily compass that tells you where to go next.

CHECK-IN

One way of working with creativity is to regularly take the temperature of where you are, noting in detail any changes and fluctuations in your emotional responses.

Attempt now to listen to yourself – search for your heartbeat. What do you hear?

This technique can also be transferred to a group context.

Often our stuckness is reinforced by a negative environment – a small town, a family, a job.
In these circumstances, a group version of taking the temperature (a check-in) is essential.

A check-in can be done in many ways.

Try –

- Numbers 1–10
- Colours
- Parts of your body
- Days of the week
- Countries

as a way of identifying where you and your colleagues are within the process i.e. 'Today I'm bright red, full of positive energy' or 'I feel pale green, creative but lacking impetus'.

Surprisingly even some companies working within the creative industries can have a very uncreative approach to problem solving.

In such situations, if the block can't be interrogated, the unexplored material will get reflected back to the employees, causing all sorts of problems.

Once, whilst I was doing a check-in with a group, someone in the room fainted and the door had to be opened to let in more air.

What had been formerly repressed, the conflicts of the company, suddenly exploded like fireworks and became the focus of the session.

This gives some indication of how powerful this simple technique can be.

The group format allows something to emerge that can help to break the stalemate.

Many times a significant motif appears – something that couldn't previously be spoken about. Often, in my work, this has been a way of looking at endings, a part of Western culture that no one wants to talk about.

Conflicts, reversal, denial, opposition.

Even D.E.A.T.H.

A check-in provides a remarkable container for these shared feelings.

In extreme conditions, where the situation is really blocked, the only solution is physical activity. Avoid the tendency to stay in front of the laptop five days a week. Instead try a collective physical improvisation.

Once a month have a 'No Computer Day'. This could be a time when different lines of communication are developed –

- Face to face.
- On the telephone.
- In groups.

Act out the conflicts within the team using a gifted guest facilitator.

Allow no one to escape.

Lastly, always insist on a check-in at the start and end of any meeting.

All information is useful, wherever it appears on the scale, either positive or more critical.

If you are running a check-in, don't ignore the bad news or the good. They each have equal value.

The Exercise

Let's do a check-in now.

Use this page to choose a colour that best expresses your current mood.

Is it orange, grey, or blue; red, yellow or turquoise?

(Colour in this page.)

Attempt now
to listen to yourself – search for your heartbeat. What do you hear?

BE A RECEIVER

If you're stuck, go out into the world.

Ideas are there, in every direction you look, directed by your own seeing of the world. However, unless you actively pursue them, they will simply pass right through you, on their journey somewhere else.

Use the following list to tune in to what's out there.

Twenty Ways To Be A Receiver

- Use your wetted finger.
- Use a radio aerial.
- Use your cupped hand.
- Use your eye.
- Use a satellite dish.
- Use a soap dish.
- Use a glass.
- Use a cup.
- Use a plate, like a Frisbee.
- Use a broken TV.
- Use a broken radio.
- Use a broken video recorder.
- Use a nail file.
- Use a whisk.
- Use a fork.
- Use an old light bulb.
- Use a pen.
- Use your fingers like a web. Soak up all the forces that you can sense out there.
- Or inside you.

Remember to play, to be a child.

After all, none of these things can really work, can they?

Treat this exercise as if it were a performance. To do some of these activities you will need to step into the space, to be more visible. Don't be afraid. Instead, use your body to demonstrate to everyone present, even in a public place, that you are prepared to take a risk.

Likewise it's very important that you make yourself visible. Start saying, 'I'm here. I'm ready to be creative.' Often this simple act of self-determination can change your direction.

A few years ago, I learned this lesson in a very interesting manner.

I was the artist on a large-scale residency, at a well-known newspaper. In my original pitch, I proposed that I adapt the lighting of their office building to create a particular mood.

Unfortunately, there were objections and rather than fight for the idea, I acceded and took another, less quarrelsome route.

I didn't ask for what I really wanted and so was thwarted.

Incidentally, the alternate plan I submitted for the residency didn't work either.

I always find that by compromising your idea, it becomes diluted and therefore less satisfying to everyone else out there. Your lack of confidence gets mapped onto the world around you.

If this happens, bring the difficulty of the work into the finished product. It's this complicated dialogue between you and the challenge that can eventually represent your time there.

Ask for what you want, be bold, persuasive – only then can you begin to get what you require.

Otherwise, how do I know what you need?

Ask for what you want – only then can you begin to get what you require.

BRICK WALL

How do you get through a brick wall?

The easiest way is to drive right through. However, take a more intelligent route. Push each brick out, until a small space appears.

Creativity is exactly the same. You don't need to see the whole journey ahead in order to advance. Instead, just clear away the bricks, one at a time, to mark a future path.

It's only this slight shift in perception that you are hoping to effect, in order to blow up the blockade.

The Exercise

Think about your current barriers.

Are you –

- Anxious.
- Lacking resources.
- Unconfident.
- Without structure?

Take some A4 paper and cut out simple brick shapes from the page.

Write the barriers, as many as you like, one on each brick, then lay them on the floor in the form of a wall.

Does anything strike you?

See what happens if you remove one brick from the structure, like the word 'Unconfident'. Alternatively, keep 'Unconfident' and instead remove 'Lacking resources'.

Or take both away from the wall.

How does that alter things?

In another version of this exercise, I allow participants to substitute new bricks into the façade –

- Money
- Collaborators
- Rope
- Organisation
- Magic

to see how these arrivals change things.

If you eradicate 'Anxious' with the new word 'Collaborators', what's the outcome?

When I ran a workshop in Stockholm, this exercise, intended as a fragment, took up the whole day, each restaging of the wall offering another complex view of the group's boundaries.

Like a long check-in...

In this manner, you can begin to look at any barriers that exist, playfully shifting these immovable objects around, now as insignificant as kids' building blocks.

First one step and another; sometimes up, then all fall down.

You don't need to see the whole journey ahead in order to advance. Instead, just clear away the bricks, one at a time, to mark a future path.

LEAPS IN THE MIND

If you are uninspired, immediately do something different, a physical activity that might disrupt the cycle –

- Stand up.
- Make a movement.
- Look out of a window.
- Walk.
- Listen to very loud music.
- Open the door.

Or focus on stimulating one sense only.

Deprive yourself of other sensations.

Often, creative blocks become aggravated by our persistent desire for a result and our need to compete with other people. Remember, creativity is a process, not a product and not tied to output.

Instead, do something quite different to attract a less obvious solution. Become physical – this often helps. Swim, run or jump. Your answer is often far removed from the problem. So try something outside your field, to encourage a debate.

I've found that journeys by plane or train give me this distance. Looking down through the blanket of cloud, from a silver jet plane, is the perfect unconscious experience, akin to dreaming.

This method often has provocative results.

Go to a high place, like the Eiffel Tower, to get an overview, or swim in the sea to feel immersed. Try a journey on the Bullet Train if you want to accelerate, or sharpen a knife to cut through.

Strangely, the intention to do these things – to go to Japan or Paris – actually activates something in you that can give proven, accurate results.

Making leaps in the mind.

It's true that a change in geography can't alter pre-existing psychological conditions; however it can make a shift in your thinking.

What counts is your perception of your creativity – whether you are positive or negative.

Sometimes simply placing yourself outside your own familiar four walls can have this startling, significant effect.

Top Tip
When I finished this book, I needed to add another six months on to the development period for the project to settle, for density to arrive.

Transformation only happens over time. Things can't be rushed. Life needs to occur for complexity to be present.

If necessary, let your work sit for a while.

Just wait.

Remember,
creativity is a
process, not
a product.

24 HOURS

Sometimes it's necessary to trick your mind into reducing the size of things to a scale that's more manageable.

If you get stuck, make something within one day.

Use these 24 hours to create a series of small objects that can build towards a single, larger item. As dusk arrives, string these studies together in a sequence and you will have a completed piece.

It's a perfect measure of a day…

The Exercise

Make, edit and complete something in the next 24 hours.

In this way, you can move towards a bigger idea – an exhibition, a book, a campaign – whilst convincing yourself, all the time, that you are making a less ambitious project.

If you try this method, some rules to follow are –

- Don't look back.
- Complete each day's work then set aside.
- Decide in advance your time-frame. For example, you might choose thirty days.
- At the end of this predetermined period, assess what you have made.
- Keep the best items. However, remember that these might only be one or two.

- Be rigorous in your selection methods. But until that moment, encourage everything.
- Allow all mistakes.

It's easy to fool yourself that if the right conditions were fulfilled then your creativity would surge ahead – if you had the best office, the correct materials and the latest technology. However, it's more useful to challenge this fantasy and to interrogate your own blocks, improvising with yourself in order to find a way forward.

Make something happen each and every day, using the simple materials that are to hand. Here, at least, you cannot escape.

Twenty Ways To Work With Limits

- Create dots or words on a page. Join them up.
- Make small, make multiple.
- Make creative projects like a trail to be followed.
- Make work every day.
- Start at daybreak, finish by dusk.
- Allow process.
- Work with the breath.
- Work until you are physically exhausted.
- Work with physical limitations.
- Work in an unfamiliar practice for a week. What have you learned?
- Work with physical exercise – kick the ball.
- Work as on a tightrope. Focus on each step.
- Work in ten minutes.
- Do a doodle.
- Make a model or maquette of the bigger thing.
- Make work in your front room or your kitchen.

- Creativity doesn't actually exist until it finds physical form.
- Work in a notepad but make what you write or draw the finished versions.
- Simply tear them out of the book and pin them to the wall.
- Exhibit it just like that.

Top Tip

One of the paradoxical elements of creativity is that the work we have so lovingly crafted often needs to be destroyed in order to move forward.

Unless we do this, everything remains stale.

Likewise, if you have finished a project and are ready to output it, but feel that something is not quite right, trust your instinct.

Be unafraid.

Remake everything, even right up until the last minute.

Start at dawn
and complete
your work
before dusk.

8

USE COLOUR

- Use colour to bypass static thinking.
- Let it access your less intellectual self.
- Invoke the impulses of a child through crayon and paint, felt-tip and acrylic.

USE COLOUR

Colour is a good way of addressing an intellectual impasse.

Write a daily diary that recounts all the good experiences, and the bad ones, through a filter of colour.

Build –

- Yellow cloud.
- Bright experience.
- Grey horizon.

Make these colour charts the content and tone of your work.

I once had an artist come to see me. It quickly became clear that her practice was about the substance of water, so I suggested that she follow the river, the Thames, observing it every day, creating maps of these long journeys.

If necessary, follow your feelings all the way back to the source.

Where does that take you?

Top Tip
Choose a colour to work with as the main ingredient for a series of works – your 'Blue Period' or your 'Red Years'.

Red Ears.

Colour is
a good way of
addressing an
intellectual
impasse.

9

CONVERSE WITH BLOCKS

- Talk to the block.
- Allow it to have the space that was previously denied.
- Destroy all sense of the difference between 'you' and 'it', so beginning a useful dialogue.

CONVERSE WITH BLOCKS

Once, an artist came to see me, asking how to release his pent-up creativity.

His practice had ground to a halt two years earlier and he was making no more work. Even his notepad was empty.

He admitted to me that he had no time to write.

My only solution to this problem was to suggest working with creativity every day. Creative blocks can easily be disinterred but they can only be dismantled piece by piece, each 24 hours.

What I meant by this was that in order to release something of the frozen feeling, he needed to bring his attention back to himself, investigating the source of the problem.

I suggested working with the image of a house – the dwelling representing the persona, the self.

You can't solve the block by –

- Shopping.
- Making money.
- Travelling.
- Moving home.

If you do that, the difficulty will always come back. Instead, peel away the layers until you reveal what's really at the core.

- Find a crack.
- Build a gap.
- Make a hole.

A disjuncture, a fracture, creates a space for something new to emerge, something we hadn't thought of before.

Try the methods below for cutting through the block.

Twenty Ways Of Working With A Block

- Write about the block.
- Ask it questions.
- Describe the block as an island, a room, a country. Go to that place.
- Take it to the supermarket.
- Use words to make cuts or chinks in the armour of the block.
- Throw a rope out of the pit that you have fallen into and haul yourself out.
- Cut a hole in the block and look through to the other side.
- Place a chair for it at the table. However, once you are ready to leave the block behind, put the chair outside the room.
- Draw the block.
- Invest the block in some minor object, like a newspaper, then discard it in a public place.
- Shrink the block in size, then put it in the wastebasket.
- Use volume to overwhelm the block.
- Say 'I am creative' very loudly several times.
- Destroy the block with a single, accurate word.
- Shoot the problem with an imaginary gun.

- Never ignore the block.
- Ignoring it will make it furious, delinquent.
- Instead be kind to the problem.
- Try to understand it.
- The block is always, inevitably, the answer to the block.

Once the authority of the block can be interrogated, just a fraction, it will disappear.

Robbed of value, it must vanish.

Top Tip
Get into conversation with the block.

Ask it open-ended questions –

- How do you feel?
- What do you want?
- How can I help?

In this way, the to and fro of practice will become actualised every day, making small moves, slowly, one at a time, each a minor step forward.

The block is
always the
answer to the
block.

BOREDOM

Instead of only experiencing difficulty, invite this element into your work.

Write your own sentence here:

'I am bored with X.'

In fact, boredom is a very helpful quality. It indicates that the techniques that you have successfully used up until now are redundant. They don't work any more.

So you have ground to a halt.

Your bored feelings are what you need to interrogate in order to move ahead.

One trick that I have found useful in expelling boredom is to work with your own perceptions, focusing on what you see and hear in your immediate surroundings.

Describe or draw these elements in microscopic clarity.

Keep going for hours, or days, until the inertia shifts.

If you have nothing to say, describe –

- Your hand.
- Your smell.
- Your tongue in your mouth.
- Your gait.

- Your sensation of your skin.
- Your mental processes.
- Your image in the mirror.

Continue until you feel something change.

In this manner, you are using the very things that you are bored with – your body, your room, your appearance, your environment – to generate new material. But don't worry about feeling negative. That's also OK.

Accept that you can only work slowly, inching forward, as if on a precipice, a ledge.

That's how creativity always is.

I also suggest writing a daily 'Boredom Diary', one in which all the minor irritations, anger, lassitude, disruptions and false dawns find an appropriate place.

Put in it –

- Things you fear.
- Things you half remember.
- Things you have destroyed.
- Things you observe from the car window.
- Things you need urgently.
- Things you have left behind.
- Things you touch by accident.
- Things you buy, not needing.
- Things you affect.

Don't hide. Don't be afraid of putting yourself in the picture. It's very important that you make yourself visible.

Create an ‘I’ landscape where everything is you.

The penetrating insight that comes with ‘I’ is not something that we are encouraged to use very much in our culture.

It’s usually seen as egotistical.

However –

- My eyes
- My mouth
- My voice
- My touch
- My ears

are always the way forward in creativity.

The Exercise

Explore your own boredom in all its detailed anxiety.

Instead of only experiencing difficulty, invite this element into your work.

CHANGE YOUR NAME

Try changing your name to create a different persona, someone who might do all the things that your ordinary self can't access.

This doesn't have to be permanent. You can try on a name change, as you might a different outfit from your wardrobe – one day a smart suit, another day a pair of jeans.

Name changes signify something. They suggest a dynamic enterprise, a new direction.

The practice of changing a name has been chosen by many artists to confirm to the outside world that it's time to be something different.

Some of my favourites are –

- Le Corbusier.
- Mother Theresa.
- Voltaire.
- Confucius
- Judy Chicago.
- Rrose Sélavy
- Cousin It.
- Lulu.

One word names are especially good. Also, names ending with an 'o' are very effective, suggesting a universality of approach.

Try on different names, one for each project, in order to give yourself a new edge, another possibility.

What would be the one word that sums up your new self?

Once, one of my colleagues was very stuck. She had moved to a new town and was feeling bored and listless. I suggested that the next day she should take a train to the nearest big city and spend a few hours there in the character of a different persona.

This new identity was able to embody all the wildness and energy that her ordinary self couldn't access.

And allowed a breakthrough.

Top Tip
In my career, I've also sometimes been drawn to the use of group names as a form of subterfuge.

The collective can offer me a form of protection.

'ARP', 'Balloon', 'E.N.A.M.' (all group identities).

Even if the name is an invention, I can hide under its umbrella, implying a wider scale for the work, one that is impossible to achieve as an individual.

'Anonymous' is also a useful way of putting difficult ideas out into the public arena. There's a long tradition of using this device to subvert political hierarchies.

Use a disguise if you need it.

Try on different names, one for each project, in order to give yourself a new edge, another direction.

BECOME INVISIBLE

As I've previously noted, the difficult side of creativity is the threat of exposure – the challenge of showing work to others.

This part is easy to ignore. However, be careful. I have seen many people crumble under the weight of adverse criticism or poorly judged advice.

Build up your defences in order to shield what's valuable to you.

(Don't give your power away.)

The exercises in this book are designed to encourage creativity. However, be careful to protect yourself from over-enthusiastic openness.

I suggest only going as far as you feel able and never pushing yourself beyond what feels comfortable.

In time you will be able to risk more, but take it slowly.

Often we don't realise that we are exposing a more vulnerable side until it's too late. Think through any context where you are likely to show your work –

- A gallery.
- A board meeting.
- An exhibition.
- A pitch.

Find an appropriate structure that offers an antidote to these stressful environments.

Sometimes, after a period of being seen, it's useful to become invisible – in order to restore your precious resources. On these occasions, a time of retreat is absolutely necessary.

Ignore the crowd.

Ignite your super powers and shroud creativity in an invisible cape.

Switch off the mobile phone, unplug the laptop, delete the email.

Wander the city alone, following your curiosity, always remaining quietly unseen.

The Exercise

Arrange your outputs, bit by bit, so that the only part visible is what's currently showing.

Box the rest.

Don’t give your power away.

10

RANDOMISE

- Roll the dice.
- Use these means to add unpredictability to your work.
- Allow other systems to override your practice, taking away the authority of the artist's hand.

RANDOMISE

Creativity is not a linear journey but a circular event, returning to the same context over and over again, each time reapproaching it from a slightly different angle.

Artistic life therefore becomes a zigzag through these different emotional states, like a ball bearing bouncing inside a pinball machine, each time responding to the force of contact.

It doesn't move from A–Z but from B–X or P–F, via G.

Yet, once you accept that creativity is necessarily unpredictable, it's possible to make the erratic quality of the process an advantage by amplifying its capricious nature.

Do this by using random properties –

- Coins.
- The shake of the dice.
- Cut-ups.
- Names taken from a hat.

The Exercise

Place a series of phrases into a paper bag. Tear them up, so they look like strips of confetti.

Use the words: 'maps', 'exaggerate', 'white', 'summer', 'backwards', 'child', 'go to', 'mountain', 'I see', 'you', 'exonerate', 'dusk', '1pm', 'bluebird'.

Or invent your own sentences (it can be as abstract as you like).

Pick them out of the bag, one at a time, writing the texts in your notepad.

What do you discover?

I've used this method all the way through my creative career and I've never found any context that couldn't be improved by this randomising technique.

The consequences are often surprising. It might not be that the outcome of this exercise generates a finished product but the process stimulates a new way of thinking about your creativity – turning what was previously safe and solid material into something fluid and indeterminate.

The reason why this method is so effective is that it encourages us to lose control; to break down the 'us' that we have worked so hard to assemble – to push through to a deeper sense of ourselves, beyond the markers of time and place.

- Aleatory practice.
- Random choices.
- Chaotic principles.

These techniques tune you into the collective unconscious – a cluster of sensory perceptions, beyond the control of language; a world of not-self, outside the defences of the ego.

The collective unconscious (Jung's invention) can be channelled through these simple methods, pulling each of us into a deeper reality, one not limited by boundaries of body or space.

- Coins.
- Toys.
- Dice.

These simple devices build a bridge between the individual and the collective.

Sometimes, I've used randomness as a methodology in my work. However, it's more likely that these elements come into my creative life through my surroundings, serendipitously flickering on the outskirts of my consciousness.

- An unexpected colour.
- Sounds from my neighbour's headphones.
- A malfunctioning LED display.
- Wrong turnings down a city street.

These events have arrived so many times in my working practice that I now see them as trophies, indications that I am tuned into my own creativity. The more they occur the better I feel.

Top Tip
Watch out for randomness in the most prosaic of situations – the lights in a building at night, the roar of airplanes overhead and the spilled tickets on a railway station floor.

The chaotic is everywhere you look.

Creativity is not a linear journey but a circular event, returning to the same context over and over again.

2CG

I decided to call up Carl Gustav Jung to see what guidance he might have to offer.

After all, I'm very influenced by his approach.

However, since he's dead, I used dice to get in touch with him – as a kind of psychic telephone, a visual shorthand.

In this exercise, I presented CG with a series of options in order to let him choose the most appropriate path for me to follow.

Was the book –

- A bird (1)
- A ladder (2)
- A floor (3)
- An eye (4)
- A cliff (5)
- A fast car (6)?

I rolled the die.

Carl's reply was: (1) a bird. The answer was not, in fact, the one I was 'looking for'.

The image of a bird, with its unpredictability and range – swooping low, offering perspective – was the opposite of what I had anticipated.

Could this picture provide a route through the book, something that I hadn't already foreseen?

'Bird' was the number one idea on the list and the first thought that came into my head. Didn't that mean something?

The throw of the dice can help to legitimise decisions by us that feel intuitively correct but can't be justified by any other means. In fact, we have to fool ourselves in this way to give credibility to our innate choices.

We need the random.

I wanted to say to myself – open the map and allow yourself to travel anywhere, not just where you believe that you ought to go.

It was only through the use of the dice that I could convince myself to actually do this.

Top Tip

Innovation always comes out of misunderstanding.

If you find a word on a page that you've written that you don't feel is correct – rather than crossing it out, fold it back into the sentence.

See where it takes you.

Use this mistake to advance your creativity, fusing words together in accidental poetry.

Open the map
and allow
yourself to
travel anywhere,
not just where
you believe
that you ought
to go.

FROM THE FLOOR

Our adult lives often move us into a position of stasis, where nothing new can emerge. Creativity can give us the freedom to challenge this feeling of inevitability.

- A lack of purpose.
- Scaled-down expectations.
- A limited worldview.

Certainly the random process, with its unpredictable shifts and twists, allows us to interrogate our own stuckness and start moving again.

Randomness turns the world on its head. Values that were previously seen as unassailable, now appear out of place or old fashioned. From this vantage point, of the opposite, we can adopt a new position, more fluid and creative.

An instant way of achieving this random quality is to lie down on the floor.

The Exercise

Remember your experiments with play earlier in the book.

This time, be bolder and take the opportunity, in your office or workplace, to view a problem with the creative potential of the upside down.

Lie flat on the floor, your head completely touching the carpet. Allow your mind to float freely, adopting multiple perspectives – from both above and below.

Let your ideas wander in cartoonish landscapes and future space scenarios.

In this exercise, what appears to be the chaotic event is nothing other than the simple functioning of your unconscious, inviting you to take part in creative opportunities that you would, in the rational, upright world, have previously overlooked.

From the floor, all things appear mysterious, filled with magic.

Try to internalise this horizontal approach in all your creative thinking, without necessarily needing, on every occasion, to lie down on the floor of your office or living room.

Reflect on this radical method, checking in with your creative potential, in more upright situations -

- Meetings.
- Feedback sessions.
- Management duties.
- Supervision.

In these contexts, always remember what you learned in your time on the floor.

Top Tip
Lie down on the pavement, outside a busy station, to view your creativity from a different angle.

Here, at the level of the beggar or the child, you can watch the weather, the city and the seasons pass by.

Lie down on the floor, to view your creativity from a different angle.

CUT-UP

The cut-up, as developed by Brion Gysin, is an effective method for use within all creative endeavours. It encourages a natural randomness, a dream-like quality and is very useful when you are faced with the stubbornness and intractability of the creative block.

My version of the cut-up gets played out this way.

The Exercise

(Materials needed: scissors, paper, felt-tip pen, glue.)

Begin by writing a short paragraph about yourself. It could be a description of an event or a personal narrative.

Write the piece, double-line spaced, on a single side of a sheet of A4 paper.

- Add a colour.
- Give two adjectives.
- Include a name.

Write the statement quickly and easily. Don't labour over it. Give yourself no more than ten minutes to complete the task.

Then taking some scissors, chop up the text. This can be into groups of words or individual items. It's up to you. Again, complete this exercise rapidly, not attempting to rationalise the process.

Don't think about anything other than the immediate task in which you are engaged. Bring it back to now.

Place the cut-ups in a pile and randomly pick out a word or phrase, one at a time. Reassemble the sentences on a fresh sheet of paper. Don't try to orchestrate the results. Stick down the pieces.

Read the output as if it were an original piece of text.

- Note the discontinuities.
- Feel the rhythm.
- Sense the mood offered.

Usually, something will leap out – an odd phrase or an interesting juxtaposition. Often the first phrase that you pick from the pile becomes the title.

You might want to stop at this point. However, many times it's useful to advance to a deeper level, further articulating an idea, or a thought that comes out of the first exercise.

Write another longer description, again on double-spaced A4 paper. This time, focusing in more detail on one aspect of the previous text.

- Add microscopic clarity.
- Evoke a sense of time.
- Zoom in on one emotion.

Repeat the cut-up process exactly as before.

What happens?

This method offers you a series of complex images that can then be reintegrated into your ongoing creativity.

Try the technique alone or with a group of people intent on exploring new horizons.

Top Tip

If, as I transcribe between the page and screen, a discontinuity occurs, I always accept the result, whatever the content.

I just see this as a naturally occurring cut-up.

In this book, when I got stuck, I used another similar technique taken from Gysin's colleague, William Burroughs. Famously, when Burroughs wrote 'The Naked Lunch', he sent the chapters in random order to his publisher in Paris, who finally assembled the manuscript as if by chance.

Likewise, I randomised parts of my text to reveal unusual relationships between the sections, ones that I hadn't seen before.

I achieved this by writing the titles on scraps of paper and pulling them out of a hat, making sure that I stuck unerringly to the order selected.

Sometimes, it's useful to physicalise an abstract idea like this, grounding it by making it happen with real objects.

Paper, light bulbs, coins, hats.

Don’t think about anything other than the immediate task in which you are engaged.

11

COPY NATURE

- Draw nature.
- Echo the variability of organic forms.
- Use these means to push yourself into spaces that are uncharacteristic and challenging.

COPY NATURE

Whilst writing this text, on a train, I used the crumbs from my sandwich that had spilt onto the notepad to determine where I should place my next sentence, thus following a wayward path across the page.

If this sounds absurd to you – don't dismiss the idea too hastily. These chance principles, drawn from nature, are often essential in cracking open the stultifying walls that can easily suffocate our creativity.

It's these games that shock us out of inertia.

For example, to avoid the stress of having to begin, write in advance some words in your notepad, then fill up the blanks with new sentences, as if you were colouring in.

Let the writing grow on the page.

Nature is a perfect model for helping us to develop a creative approach; complexity emerging from a simple seed.

Rambling, chaotic, propulsive, resistant – these are all qualities that you might want to emulate.

The best way of copying nature is to involve chance processes, allowing the techniques that I describe in this section to bring unexpected elements into your life.

Some Ways Of Copying Nature

- Be contrary in your choices.
- Double back.
- Focus on growing your practice.
- Follow the sun.
- Draw on anything you find.
- Evolve slowly.
- Be modest in your ambition.
- Stay around.

I also have toys on my desk – Flexioctons, Lego, Flash Cards etc. – objects that can be used in a modular fashion, copying the cellular structure of nature.

I play with these games to give me ideas.

However, you don't need to invest in any of these items to use this approach. Simply build bricks out of paper and write words on them, or images, then bolt the pieces back together, colliding the text in different ways –

- Loud/quiet.
- Narrative/oblique.
- Closed/open.
- Human/machine.

The most persistent problem facing people searching for their creativity is not that they can't generate material but that they believe that they don't have a big idea; so they stumble around, not having the confidence to begin.

With this chance approach, you are always beginning, always growing something.

The big idea is every day.

The Exercise

Go out now into the street and make a list of all the natural forms that you can see.

- Cloud.
- Dirt.
- Light.
- Vapour.
- Leaf.

Sketch them rapidly in your notepad.

Use these drawings as metaphorical conceits, objects that can catalyse your current process. Draw a 'dirty leaf' or 'cloudy light'.

Note: whatever strikes you first is the most important thing.

In this modular way, the world around you gets joined up in bits, every connection or link having a potential significance.

Nature is a doorway.

Whatever you see becomes the fundamental material of creativity.

Rambling, chaotic, propulsive, resistant. These are all qualities that you might want to emulate.

MICROPHONY

The tape recorder is a very effective tool for amplifying our feelings.

It makes no judgements; rather it records in a neutral way anything we put onto tape, adding volume to the slightest idea.

The Exercise

Place a microphone on your windowsill at night and download the sounds of the city into your digital recorder. Let the ideas drift into your brain as you sleep. Switch off when you wake.

In this way, allow nature to enter unfiltered into your life.

By accepting everything as it is, big and small, significant and minor, you switch off your attempts at logical control and give a voice to your under-represented emotions.

Instead of saying 'No', say 'Yes' to anything that you find.

Use the metaphor of the microphone to integrate into your creative life a wide 'gain', allowing everything to be heard.

Once I began to work in this way, I experienced a serious shift in thinking. Instead of manipulating objects into my creativity, I used what was given to me, to best effect.

I simply put into order, in a very understated way, what came to hand.

The volume of nature is also useful to work with.

For example, try overwhelming the viewer with information. Be encyclopedic. Occupy as big a space as possible, like a giant bubble, or a cloud.

Then conclude with a whisper.

Using the scale of your voice, from full volume to the barest hiss, for maximum impact.

When I was making performance work, I employed the bare bones of material – a chair, a microphone, a light – to develop ideas.

I created an intimate relationship with what I had, using the mike in a variety of complex ways, always over or under-using the object in order to create an effect.

Nothing is a very powerful tool.

Use your absence to generate a voluminous feeling, one that can't easily be denied.

Top Tip
In your work space, create a large table to display items that you have found: piles of books, flowers, objects and magazines.

Use it to build a universe in your room.

Accept
everything as
it is, big and
small, significant
and minor.

LEFT HAND

Recently I took a flight into Bordeaux to see a drawing show by artists and designers, the Bouroullec Brothers.

This long day's travel – one train, a plane, one tram and a journey on foot, reminded me of the drawn line, relentlessly pulling itself through history, a dotted series of footsteps, as determined as our own human development.

The Bouroullecs' images of blue lozenges, eccentric boulders and orange rhomboids alerted me to the fact that if we want to model creativity we should copy nature, and through this detailed process discover things about ourselves.

I was also made aware of another benefit – the process of observing nature slows us down and allows each one of us to take a breath.

Within the space of this inhalation we can see objects clearly for the first time.

In that brief gap, when we are in direct contact with the elements, unmediated by the virtual, trying to formulate a new relationship with the outside, quite lost, we really rediscover our sense of self.

We are mirrored by nature.

It's this journey; of looking and losing, of gaining and returning that is essential to creativity.

As I sat gazing out of my hotel window in Bordeaux, onto a modern thoroughfare, quite bland, a building site opposite, I wrote in my notepad continuously until the sky had changed from light grey to deep black.

Night came.

And I felt transformed.

The Exercise

Perhaps, in this instance, the traditional methods of teaching creativity by copying nature have something to recommend them.

Adapt this orthodox technique by doing something unconventional – like drawing with your left hand.

Use your pencil, creating an abstract idea of the object in front of you.

This process subverts the critical voices inside your head and allows different impressions to come through.

Or write with your left hand, letting the words tumble onto the page.

What will they say?

Observe nature,
slow down and
take a breath.

TOKYO SUBWAY

Another good technique is to allow someone else to make decisions for you. Let someone else do the choosing.

Make creative material then invite another person to organise your outputs. Develop this method to take away the authority of the artist's hand.

The clever creative understands that there are useful methodologies, external processes that can be helpful in the furthering of their own creativity.

Use –

- Clouds
- The Tokyo Subway Map
- A city grid
- Bubbles in a glass

as models for your output.

For example, take an existing map as a guide, superimposing your own text on a diagram of the Tokyo Subway. Or, conversely, create a chart from the materials that you have to hand.

Allow them to dictate a temporary narrative.

On many occasions I've thrown the *I Ching*, not just looking for an answer to a problem, but in times of difficulty surrendering myself to another system, one more knowledgeable than me.

We only know so much about our own creative process. We are all limited. Sometimes it's good to allow the disinterested hand of chance to make the decisions for us. This allows us to give up, to relinquish control.

In some cases automatism is the only solution.

The Exercise

If you are stuck, open any book at random.

Let your eye land naturally on the page and pick out the first few sentences that you see. Take the text, however bizarre, as something useful to your current predicament.

Think about the future, your next move, the following day.

Good books to try are –

- The Bible.
- A guide book.
- 'Ulysses.'
- A thesaurus.

The Dadaists named themselves by randomly stabbing a knife into a French–German dictionary and coming up with the word 'Dada'.

By using this same technique, I've always thought that I am channelling the process of Dadaism, working with their radical approach.

Twenty Ways Of Adding Random Elements

- Exhibit two opposite things together.
- Exhibit two connected things in improvised locations.
- Exhibit two ordinary things at different tempos.
- Exhibit two similar ideas simultaneously.
- Superimpose.
- Show the same few limited ideas but in many different permutations.
- Strip out the structure, leaving only bare bones.
- Exhibit the remixes, not the original.
- Show it backwards.
- Show it at half speed.
- Show it upside down.
- Show it before it's complete.
- Show the back of it.
- Make one major part of your work an obvious blunder.
- Make one major part of your work unpredictable.
- Make one major part of your work full of human errors.
- Reverse the order, starting at the end.
- Reverse the dynamic, starting with the loudest.
- Reverse the sense, starting with the most obscure line.
- Work forwards, towards clarity.

Top Tip

Go back to an old text, one that you haven't read for twenty years. Make a mental note of all your underlinings, your emphases, your scribbles in the margins.

Or, alternatively, only buy second-hand books.

Use other people's written notes and dedications to construct a new narrative for you to inhabit.

Let someone else do the choosing. Let someone make decisions for you.

12

LOSE THE EGO

- Work within a group context.
- Draw resources from this alternate power supply.
- Make a new you, unfettered by the rules of personality or history.

LOSE THE EGO

In my own work, when I get stuck, I always ask other practitioners to contribute an idea or to make an intervention.

All my early experiments in art were with sound and the collaborative nature of music making, especially within the electronic avant-garde, has stayed with me until the present day.

I often think of images and text as audio streams and this technique enables me to look at the material in a fluid way, not bounded by rules or structure.

If the process can remain an improvisation, right up to the last minute, or even within the performance, then more things are possible.

Who says that the work must be fixed?

I keep an LP record by experimental composer Christian Wolff next to my hi-fi to remind myself of this fact.

I've found it a great relief, after years of making solo projects, when I've taken part in group events where everyone contributes equally. In these forums, I'm not trying to control the context so I can merge successfully with the collective, surrendering, in part, my individual identity.

The group is a powerful machine. It's like the sun.

It can sustain, nurture and develop. You put a limited amount of energy in and more comes out at the other end.

(((((O)))))

(The sun.)

It's a very satisfying experience.

The Exercise

Is your ego in control?

I wonder what might happen if something was different, if you lost all power supply to the brain?

A way of achieving this is to focus on not being the lead creative but instead playing at being the assistant. Allow the controlling mind to take a back seat, abandoning your usual sense of self.

Through these means create holes in your identity (like gunshots in a firing range score card), letting space flow through.

If you can encourage this concept of service into your working life, many changes will occur, mysterious options, all closely tied to the idea of surrender.

Recently, when working collaboratively on generating audio material for a live event, I was forced to listen to others in the room, so as not to overwhelm proceedings.

In fact, the situation improved when I abandoned my usual role and simply placed microphones around the studio, recording what was occurring elsewhere, on the fringes.

The egoless position of an assistant, facilitating a process, enabled a stronger sense of cooperation to be present.

I realised that things always work best in reduction.

Listening and tuning in, reflecting and finding space: this is usually the most effective methodology.

I often find that when these boundaries of the self dissolve, the output also becomes slippery, exotic, as if the content also disintegrates. In these moments, all ideas float into view, boundaryless, benign.

So much so that we kept the tape recorder running and left the room, letting the sound take its own idiosyncratic path.

Top Tip
Develop relationships through more informal networks.

Take away the formality of the hierarchy and invite some colleagues out to lunch. Meetings are easier, simpler and more effective when convened over a shared meal.

The chicken leg, the tofu sandwich and the cheese board are all vehicles for transformation.

You pay.

Lose the ego – drop all power supply to the brain.

CALL OUT MY NAME

It's possible to enlarge your creativity by building a dialogue with other collaborators, drawing on their internal qualities.

It doesn't matter whether they are unknown or famous, alive or dead. Simply concentrate on the innate characteristics that they represent.

Call out to them, using their name, asking for help.

'John...'
'Marshall...'
'Bruno...'
'Yoko... '

(These are my names.)

What qualities do you need from them?

Are they –

- Stability
- Indifference
- Excitement
- Detail
- Authority
- Chaos
- Impertinence
- Resolve
- Danger

or calm?

It's possible to create a whole piece of work based around these calls to qualities. You could title it 'To X' and base the study around written and spoken invocations of your chosen recipients' subtle characteristics.

Likewise, call on the collective unconscious for help, as if you were dialling for a pizza. Pick up the phone and imagine that you are talking to someone at the other end who can grant your wishes. Have an imaginary conversation with them.

Ask for anything you need to develop your creativity.

- Images.
- Planning.
- Ideas.

Call the Big Pizza Man in the sky and see what he sends you.

In the next few days, on the street, keep your eyes and ears open, to see what he will deliver.

The Exercise

Write down the creative elements that are missing inside you.

In the top half of the next page, draw any conflicts that currently exist in your artistic life, whilst below the line, draw any solutions, however abstract, to these current dilemmas.

Call on the collective unconscious for help, as if you were dialling for a pizza.

16

Try to remember what you were interested in when you were sixteen. Bring these years back into your current life.

At sixteen, on the cusp of adulthood, coming into self-awareness, anything that holds our attention is useful to recall.

Step back into this period of your life and see where it takes you. Slow yourself down to 16 rpm, like a record on a turntable.

Investigate the grooves of the disc, slowly passing by. You are the rings, the shiny acetate, the concentric circles, the annual memories of a tree as it spins you back into the past.

What you are hoping for with this exercise is to reconnect with your enthusiastic former self, a more mobile form, less predictable than your current incarnation, and so remind you of your original impetus.

The world of the forming personality is a useful territory to investigate.

- TV.
- Sleep.
- Darkened bedroom.
- Summer.
- Hot cream.

Return to the crucible of your earliest thoughts.

After all, the ironic persona that you presently adopt is only a part of who you are. Dig deeper, under the surface, to the innate, enthusiastic self that knows no boundaries and few limits.

Use the flashbacks in your brain – the giant library inside you – to assemble new stories from the material that you find there.

- A memory.
- A sense of place.
- A remembered colour.
- A city street.

You don't need inspiration outside yourself, instead use the vast range of experiences that you already have, to fill in the blanks.

Top Tip
In the same serendipitous way that you might collect random objects on the street, to make something creative, use the personality in a similar manner.

Merging and colliding, fusing and crushing.

Age 16, 35, 8, 19, 44, 67.

Jump to and fro in time, imagining every version of yourself that you care to be.

Slow yourself
down to 16 rpm,
like a record on
a turntable.

TUNING OUT

Since I spent the opening parts of the book talking about ways of tuning into creativity, it would be useful now, as you approach the end of the volume, to discuss how you might tune out.

What's the best way of turning off your internal radio?

This is not as difficult as you might imagine. Every day, each one of us rehearses this ending by going to sleep – surrendering to a world of absence, a place not inhabited by our conscious mind.

As a result, I find these last few moments before I drop off, charged with electricity. In the white noise of vacant meandering, losing myself, untrapped by the ego, I have some of my best ideas.

Freed from logic, my mind makes indecipherable maps and I put these down in a notepad that I keep by my bed for this exact purpose,

- 'Cone.'
- 'White book.'
- '7.12.'
- 'Cut here.'

(Ideas that never made it into this text.)

The elements that occur on the edge of sleep are often the upside down solutions to long-term creative problems, locked safe in the capsule of your head, only to emerge at night-time, when all reason collapses.

Instructions: don't listen to the critical voices inside you but write down anything that drops into your brain. All these jagged words ultimately mean something and can find a use.

So, don't throw them away.

Sometimes, I find the particular concept that I need comes from beyond my ego –

- An accidental slip-up.
- A suggestion from a surprising source.
- A visual mismatch.
- A shift to another physical environment.

The solution is always in the backward glance, as you leave the problem behind to go somewhere else.

In a car, being driven in a taxi, on a train, at the airport.

In between spaces – where the upside down can take hold.

And surprise you.

The solution is always in the backward glance, as you leave the problem behind to go somewhere else.

SLEEP

Sometimes sleep is the only answer.

If you are at an impasse, spend a couple of days resting or padding around your flat, waiting for a sign to come.

This might be a call at the door, a barely remembered book or an image that you see out of the window.

Pay attention, in a half-asleep way, and something will turn up. An idea will emerge out of your involuntary mind to blast the log-jam.

Cook a dinner, listen to the radio and daydream.

Abandon the life of your logical mind and surrender to the illogic of castaway thoughts. Record your dreams but only in a haphazard way, as if with your eyes half-closed.

Illness is also of benefit to the artist – a period of malady often heralds a shift, a move forward. Do not resist the heightened awareness that this infection can bring.

Fever or hallucination can substantially develop your powers of perception and allow a mental leap into new territory.

In my essay 'Dusk' (2006) I discuss how these parasitic experiences can actually enhance our personal vision, offering a deeper sense of identity.

In reality, you have little control over your creative output. Of course you can add systems and processes etc. just as we have discussed in this book, but really you have no chance to change anything.

Sometime it's good to remember this fact.

Instead, allow found objects to have an impact on your life.

Choose at random –

- A TV channel.
- A book.
- A shortwave radio station.
- An old magazine.

Within the world of the automatic, you will be able to find all that you need, direct from your own resources.

Dream and note down, in microscopic detail, all the journeys that you make in your head at night.

Use it...and

sleep.

In reality, you have little control over your output.

12 RULES OF CREATIVITY

1 Open Your Eyes.

2 Prepare The Space.

3 Play.

4 Use Images.

5 Do The Opposite.

6 Develop Failure.

7 Check-In.

8 Use Colour.

9 Converse With Blocks.

10 Randomise.

11 Copy Nature.

12 Lose The Ego.

12 RULES OF CREATIVITY

The 12 rules of creativity, which I have described here, in this volume, are a process-based system, alerting you to different techniques that you might use to develop your creativity.

It's a practical methodology. If you take one thing away from the reading of this book, it should be that creativity, as it manifests within you, is always possible.

Go ahead: do it.

However, there is no simple route to a new life and no creative renewal without difficulty.

Transformation only comes through changes in you.

A pencil is used not only to draw pictures but to create a distinct outline around ourselves, colouring us in.

Yet, considering that this process is not without its difficulties, I often ask myself why we start on this journey.

I believe that the answer is that we do it in order to explore our fears – pushing at the boundary of creativity in order to engage with risk.

The task is challenging.

(It's a lifetime's work).

So –

- Give yourself enough time.
- Give yourself enough resources.
- Give yourself enough space.

Be unafraid to ask for these, if you need them. There's nothing silly or slight about these demands.

Please, be compassionate towards yourself.

I encourage you to love the products that you make – for surely that is the aim of the higher arts, to enlarge our experience through tenderness and awareness, intellect and clarity.

Do not underestimate the level of visibility that will be needed in order to make your projects real. (You will be standing on a stage, lit by a bright spotlight, whether you want to or not.) However, it's partly through this willing exposure to danger that we extend ourselves, grow into new psychological spaces.

The revealing of ourselves is our catalyst.

This is the real gold, the true magic of the creative process, the power of transformation.

You are the output.

Many times, I admit, I have given up and retreated from creativity. However, ultimately, I have returned to it because I can't think of a better way for me to explore the limits of myself, other than here, on the page.

So, courage, my friend.

Make everything fresh and alive.

You are the potential that's forming every second, every minute. Make yourself the site of further explorations.

Take up your pencil and begin to write.

Start today.

Transformation only comes through changes in you.

MICHAEL ATAVAR

Michael Atavar is an artist and a creative consultant with a practice that mixes creativity, business, art and psychology.

As part of the Year of the Artist, he was the first artist in residence at the Guardian Newspaper, producing a print insert in an unlimited edition of 400,000 copies.

His output includes over thirty public works, in a variety of forms – performance, installation, digital media, publishing.

'Dusk', his last piece, was shown at the Hayward Gallery.

www.atavar.com
www.how-to-be-an-artist.com
www.12-rules-of-creativity.com
www.creativepractice.com

ACKNOWLEDGEMENTS

Several people supported this project at key stages of development – Christophe, Crispin, David, Emily, Gabrielle, Iain, Isabel, Jonathan, Judy, Julian, Laura, Leah, Martin, Neil, Nick, Nicholas, Nikki, Pascale, Pat, Peter, Portland, Richard, Ritchie, Robert, Ruth, Stella, Valerie.

Thank you to Steven Whinnery for editorial assistance and to Richard Scarborough for production advice.

Thanks to Balloon.

This book is dedicated to the memory of Norma Westhorpe.

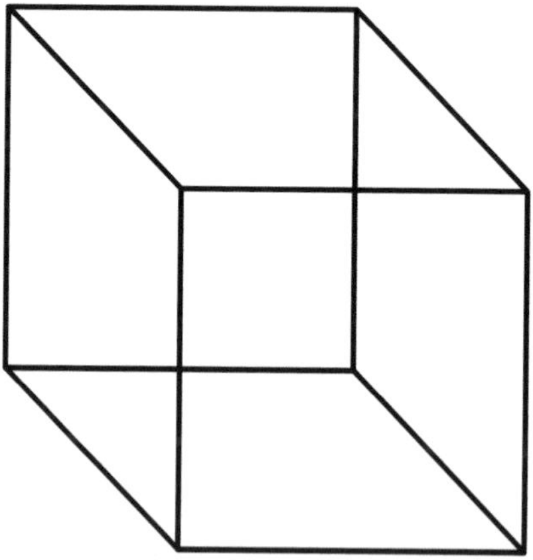

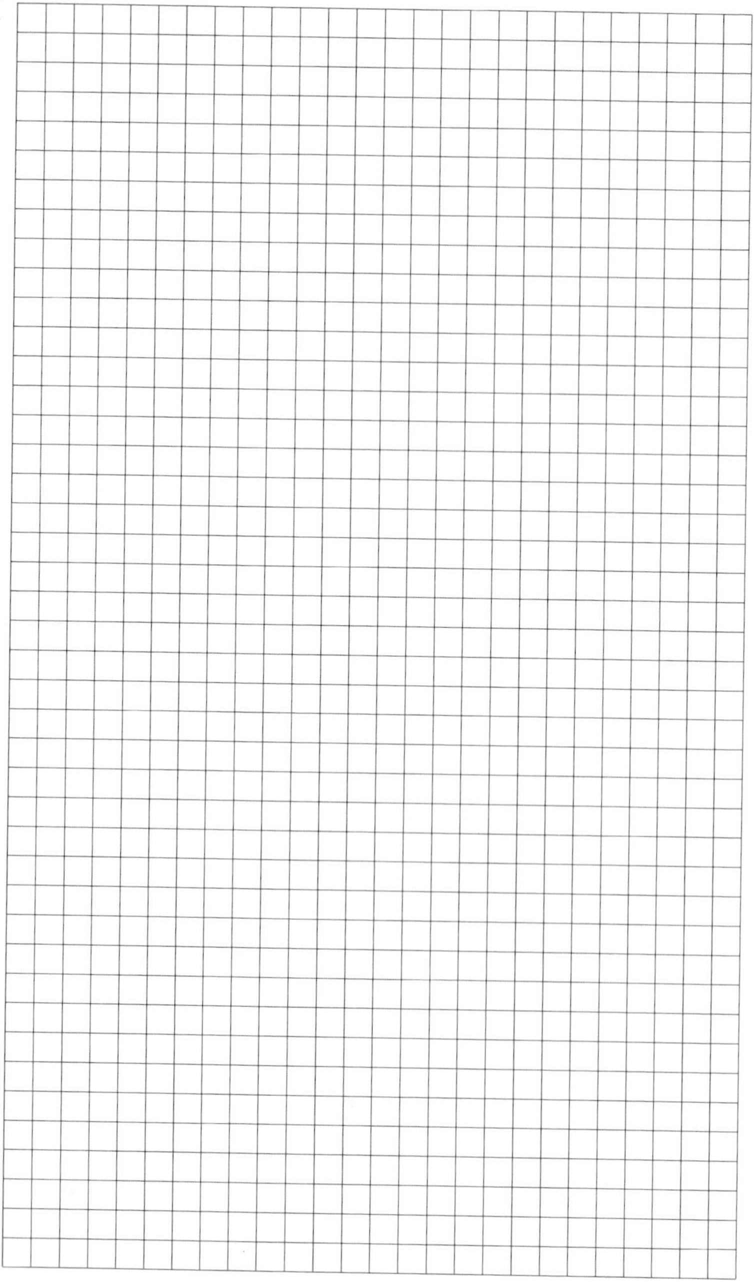

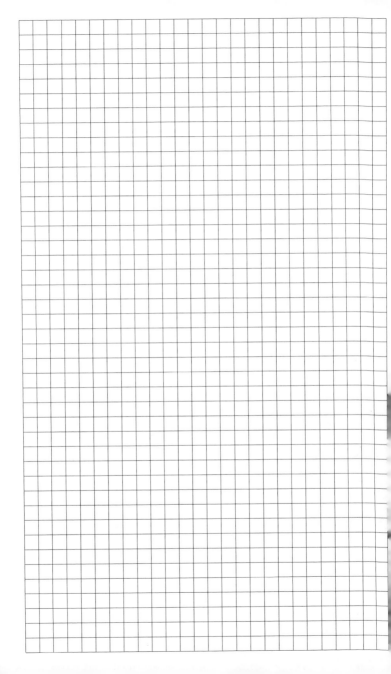

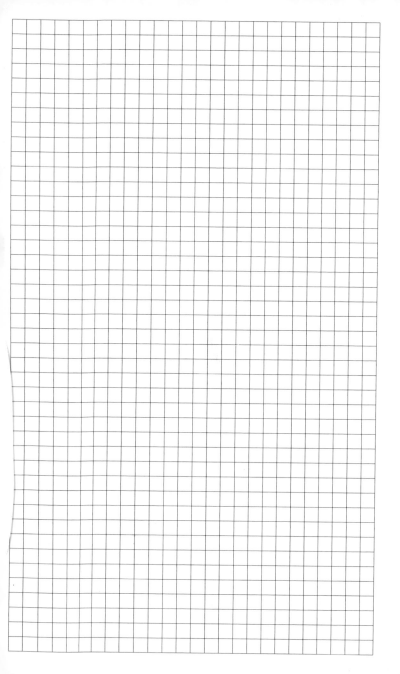